vintage
fashion
illustration

Brevit

Continental

PAULINE 59/11

BIANDO 69/11

MARQUITA 79/11

D1340943

vintage fashion illustration

From Harper's Bazaar 1930–1970

With introduction by
Marnie Fogg

BATSFORD

First published in the United Kingdom in 2010 under the title
Fashion Illustration 1930 to 1970.
This paperback edition first published in 2013 by
Batsford
10 Southcombe Street
London W14 0RA
An imprint of Anova Books Company Ltd

ISBN 9781849941129

A CIP catalogue record for this book is available from the British Library.

20 19 18 17 16 15 14 13
10 9 8 7 6 5 4 3 2 1

Reproduction by Mission Productions Ltd, Hong Kong
Printed by 1010 International Ltd, China

This book can be ordered direct from the publisher at the website
www.anovabooks.com, or try your local bookshop.

Distributed in the United States and Canada by Sterling Publishing Co., 387
Park Avenue South, New York, NY 10016, USA

Page 1: In the mid-1950s the epithet 'continental' resonated
with elegance and luxury. In this illustrated advertisement,
Brevitt sets the tone for its Continental range of stiletto-
heeled shoes in the foreground with a stylish background
figure, set on an opulent field of red. *October 1957.*

Page 2: With the definition of an architectural blueprint and
the compositional acuity of a textile design, this illustration
of rival scent bottles is a montage of cut-out line drawings
on white, mounted on a dark background and overlaid by
transparent rectangles of coloured tissue, creating an effect
of glass, set within recessed planes. *November 1956.*

Page 3: The fitted dress and strapless bodice, invariably
worn with elbow-length gloves, was a feature of 1950s
evening wear; clever foundation garments or an elaborate
substructure of built-in boning enabled the dress to remain
in place. *May 1950.*

Right: Increasing stylization and clarity of line was required
for print reproduction, as seen in these sketches using
a Rotring studio pen. Lingerie and foundation garments
were usually illustrated rather than photographed during
this time, reducing the sexual overtones of the product,
and in this case providing a whimsical playfulness that
renders the bare breasts of the figure on the right
inoffensive. *February 1967.*

Contents

Introduction

Fashion illustration is a persuasive and compelling medium that expresses not only the intentions of the designer but is also redolent of the artistic movements of the day. Resolutely of the moment, the images on the page inform, beguile and describe the fashionable image while also illustrating the prevailing archetype of female beauty. Spanning a 40-year period between 1930 and 1970, the book charts the evolution of the fashion silhouette in the context of the prevailing visual culture, from the etiolated form of the 1930s and the decorous ladylike hourglass figure of the 1950s to the cool 'dollybird' of the 1960s.

Fashion illustration evolved from the tradition of 19th-century romantic realism to being recognized as an art form in 1908, when French couturier Paul Poiret commissioned Paul Iribe to illustrate his radical new designs. Iribe interpreted this new aesthetic of exotic orientalism in a small exclusive promotional publication, *Les Robes de Paul Poiret*. This was followed in 1911 by a similar edition illustrated by Georges Lepape, *Les Choses de Paul Poiret*.

The art of fashion illustration is the result of a reciprocal relationship between the designer and the illustrator, mediated through the pages of fashion magazines, which were fundamental to the dissemination of style to an ever-increasing audience. The forerunner of the fashion magazine, *La Gazette du Bon Ton*, was launched in 1912 by publisher Lucien Vogel, in collaboration with Michel de Brunhoff, a future editor of *French Vogue*. Among the group of featured artists illustrating models from the couture houses of Poiret, Paquin and Worth were A.E. Marty, Georges Barbier, Charles Martin, J. and P. Brissaud, Paul Iribe, Georges Lepape, Umberto Brunelleschi, Pierre Morgue, Etienne Drian and Eduardo Benito. Each edition of the magazine contained up to ten colour pochoir plates and several design sketches (known as *croquis*). The *Gazette* ran from 1912 to 1914 and from 1920 to 1925, when it ceased publication and was acquired by Condé Nast, the publisher of *American Vogue* since 1893. Nast continued to use European artists as well as the established American illustrators such as George Plank, Helen Dryden, and Douglas Pollard. The relationship between fashion and art was strongest during this period: painters who were commissioned by Nast included Raoul Dufy, Magritte, Jean Dupas, Marie Laurencin, Kees van Dongen, and Robert and Sonia Delauney.

Vogue's rival publication, *Harper's Bazar*, (renamed *Harper's Bazaar* in 1929) was founded by Harper & Brothers, and in 1912 was purchased by American newspaper tycoon William Randolph Hearst. Initially launched as 'A Repository of Fashion, Pleasure and Instruction', it appeared as an upmarket weekly on 2nd November 1867 under the title *Harper's Bazar*. It wasn't until 1901 that *Harper's* became a monthly issued magazine, featuring high-quality, black-and-white engravings of London and Paris fashions, adjusted slightly to suit American taste.

In 1915 the magazine signed an exclusive contract with Russian-born fashion illustrator Erté, (Romain de Tirtoff; Erté is the French pronunciation of his initials R.T.) a collaboration that was to last until 1938, although after 1926 the artist concentrated less on fashion and more on designing for theatrical productions. The advent of modernism in the mid-1920s rendered Erté's work inappropriate for the new simplicity and androgyny of the fashions of the era. Aspects of modernism such as Cubism, Expressionism, Futurism and abstraction in painting had been in place since before World War I (1914–18) but it wasn't until the following decade that the movement influenced fashion illustration. This was manifested in the rangy, elongated silhouette of a new phenomenon – the 1920s flapper girl – who embodied the spirit of the Jazz Age and was represented by fashion illustrators such as Benito, Georges Barbier, Lepape and Benito. They expressed form and fashion in the fractional forms of Cubism and Futurism, as well as acknowledging the influence of Art Deco. This design movement began in Europe in the early years of the 20th century, though it was not universally popular until the 1925 Exposition International des Arts Decoratifs et Industriels Modernes (International Exposition of Modern Industrial and Decorative Art). It was a confluence of many trends, from the arts of Africa, Egypt and Mexico to the streamlined technology and materials of modern aviation and the growing ubiquity of the motor car of the 'speed age'.

Rivalry between the two main fashion magazines of the period, *Vogue* and *Harper's Bazaar*, was intensified when pioneer fashion photographer Adolphe de Meyer was poached from *Vogue* by William Hearst in 1922, leading to a greater emphasis on the use of photography within its pages. This was followed by the appointment of another *Vogue* talent, Carmel Snow, who became editor-in-chief of the magazine in 1932. By this time, de Meyer's ethereal, studio-centred style that utilized backlighting and gauze-covered lenses began to lose its appeal, and he was usurped by the graphic design genius Alexey Brodovitch, appointed by Snow as art director of the magazine in 1934. Brodovitch revolutionized magazine design during his time at *Harper's Bazaar*, with his innovative use of white space and cinematic organization of layout.

Rather than displaying the whole garment, the designer often incorporated his signature cropping technique on the figure and manipulated the shape of the text to reflect the forms within a photograph or illustration. At a time when colour was unusual in magazines, he used a single second colour in contrast to black to great effect. Brodovitch's earlier experiences in his Parisian design studio prompted him to continually import ideas and artists from Europe. Among the artists that worked for *Bazaar* were Jean Cocteau, Raoul Dufy, Leonor Fini, Marc Chagall, Man Ray and A.M. Cassandre, the most eminent poster artist in France at the time, replacing the former cover favourite, Erté. At the height of the Surrealist movement, artists Salvador Dali and de Chiroco were commissioned.

Although illustrators were much in demand from the leading journals of the three fashion capitals of New York, Paris and London during the 1930s, the deployment of illustration began to be challenged by the photographic work of Steichen, Horst, Hoynigen-Huene, Beaton and Man Ray. Editorial and advertorial content in the magazines diverged, resulting in advertisers depending on illustration to sell their goods, while the photographic image gradually replaced illustration on the fashion pages, particularly on the covers of the magazines. The first colour cover photograph for *Vogue* by Edward Steichen appeared in 1932, and by 1936 it was deemed by the publishers that a photographed cover sold more copies than one that was illustrated. From this period the work of artists and photographers began to be used side by side within the editorial body of the magazine, only shifting in emphasis after 1950, when the use of photography became paramount.

The influence of the Art Nouveau and the Art Deco movement still resonated throughout the 1930s until American-born Carl Erikson, known as Eric, and Rene Bouet-Willaumez, or RBW, brought a new realism to fashion illustration. They instigated a style of illustration that recognized the importance of drawing from life, and both were first and foremost artists, rather than illustrators. Rivals and regular contributors for *Vogue*, Eric's preferred medium was charcoal. He deployed accurate observation, an elegant line, loose brushwork and colour washes, while RBW preferred to use a pen. French painter and portraitist Rene Bouche added his calligraphic style and Christian Berard, who also had a background in fine arts and theatre, initially worked for *Harper's Bazaar* before moving to *Vogue*.

In 1947, Parisian couturier Christian Dior (1905–57) unveiled his Corolle line, later dubbed by journalists as the New Look. It changed the shape of fashion for a decade and defined the dominance of that city as the elite of the post-war fashion industry. It was an era when the fashion consumer was in thrall to the dictates of couturiers such as Christian Dior, Jacques Fath, Cristobel Balenciaga, Pierre Balmain and Hubert Givenchy. The twice-yearly fashion shows in Paris were reported by the press to an eagerly waiting consumer as well as to a burgeoning mass-production industry and were recorded for various magazines by illustrators Rene Bouche, Eric, RBW, Berard, Bernard Blossac, Gruau, Demachy, Tom Keogh, and Francis Marshall.

The death of Eric in 1958, and Bouche five years later, marked the end of illustration as the major means of fashion communication. During this period the focus shifted from the art of the cover to the model and her clothes, aesthetics being less important than the business of selling a product. From this period onwards, illustration was used for lingerie (photography being considered too risqué for such a subject), apart from certain specialist campaigns such as Rene Grau' scent campaign for Christian Dior. His style was reminiscent of Mucha and Toulouse-Lautrec and he was one of the first illustrators to be identified with advertising, mainly for Christian Dior.

Fashion illustration was also used by trade magazines such as *International Textiles* and *L'Officiel de la Modeet du Couture*. In the United States John Fairchild's *Women's Wear Daily*, which he had successfully revamped in 1960 to make it the most influential of the fashion press, employed Kenneth Paul Block, Stipleman, Pedro Barrios, Perleman, and Stephen Melendez.

The youth culture of the 1960s democratized fashion. As the clothes became more stylized, so too did the illustrations; the proliferation of fashion media at the time demanded an ease of reproduction which included the possibility of scaling the image down, requiring clear details of the garments. These appeared on the pages of the new magazines for teenagers such as *Honey* (1961) and *Petticoat* (1966) in the UK and American 'teen' magazines. High fashion was mediated through the lens of the celebrity photographers and their models in the pages of *Vogue* and *Harper's Bazaar*. Eric Stemp and Angela Landels continued to draw in the style sustained by the life class, but it was the work of a single fashion artist that caused the art of fashion illustration to be reappraised and rejuvenated. Born in Puerto Rico, Antonio Lopez (1943–1987) dominated fashion illustration from the mid-1960s. Antonio's influential flamboyant and exuberant style rendered fashion illustration once again a vital form of expression, providing inspiration to a new generation of artists.

1930s

TWO SHILLINGS NETT

HARPER'S BAZAAR

INCORPORATING "VANITY FAIR"

SEPTEMBER
1930

FURS
AND
FABRICS

COSMETICS

Previous page: Pencil drawing by Sladelucas depicting the effectiveness of shading in representing the tactile bias-set bands of ermine in a simple wrap coat. An example of the documentary style of fashion illustration. *March 1933.*

Left: Leon Bénigni (1892–1948) was a draftsman, lithographer and illustrator. His greatest commercial success was as a posterist, the most famous being *Brides les Bains*, (1929). The stylized monochrome couple offset against the broad red vertical stripes and the simple geometric line drawing of the chauffeured motor car evidence the continuing influence of Art Deco. *September 1930.*

Right: Pre-eminent fashion artist Reynaldo Luza (1893–1978) was born in Lima, Peru. In 1921 he joined *Harper's Bazaar* as the principal fashion artist, a position he was to hold for 27 years. This image includes a broad set of references from Matisse to Hokusai. *October 1930.*

Previous page: The fashionable bathing costumes of the era allowed the illustrator to disseminate images of near nudity, which paved the way for more liberating clothes, as in these designs by fashion house Paul Caret. The concentric circles of the hats designed by milliner Madelon Chaumet form a pleasing composition with the vertical stripes of the garments and the horizontal stripes of the umbrella. *July 1930.*

Left: Eric Fraser (1902–1983) made a major contribution to the art of illustration. His output included cartoons and caricatures, designs for posters and Christmas cards, and fashion illustrations including many for *Harper's Bazaar.* The background to the two figures fuses an enigmatic cityscape redolent of de Chiroco with the naive foliage of Rousseau's primitivism. *January 1931.*

Right: The simplicity of line and minimal expression of this head is depicted in the style of Romanian sculptor Constantin Brâncusi, whose work included the influential *Sleeping Muse* (1910). *April 1931.*

Right: Kenneth Crouch illustrates the archetypal silhouette of the era: a small, neat head and etiolated body that typified the ladylike elegance of 1930s fashions. The *ombréd* vertical stripes of the background provide contrast to the vertical lines of the pleated dresses. *November 1930.*

Left: Fashion illustration was the only means of communicating to a wide audience the work of the French couturiers such as Charles Worth, Callot Soeurs and Jeanne Paquin. The architectural treatment of the drapery is captured here by illustrator Kenneth Crouch. *May 1931.*

Right: The perspective of this image recognizes the Renaissance tradition of confining the landscape to the extreme bottom edge of the picture, so that the figures are silhouetted against the sky and held within a frame of overarching cherry blossom. *April 1930.*

Above: American painter, designer and illustrator Carolyn Edmundson (born 1906) evokes the atmosphere of an Edward Hopper painting in this illustration, comprised of darkly brooding colours and the sense of catching a moment in time. *January 1932.*

Right: The details of the garments are subsumed to the impact of Bénigni's overall design in this cover; the reclining figure forms a compelling juxtaposition of colourful shapes, rather than providing information about the model's clothes, and reflects the modernism of the title's sans serif font. *July 1931.*

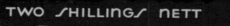

TWO SHILLINGS NETT

HARPER'S BAZAAR

INCORPORATING "VANITY FAIR"

ULY 1931

SUMMER
TRAVEL
NUMBER

Left and right: Eric Fraser displays his consistent mastery of organizing multiple images to great effect in this beach scene. The cropped figure on the left and the seated model on the right contain a scene that is alive with movement and detail. *July 1931*.

Left: All about texture; this image by Malaga Grenet literally draws parallels between the lustrous locks of hair and the tactile fur collar. *September 1931.*

Right: The painterly evocation of these three evening gowns by Scottish-born illustrator Anna Zinkeisen evidences her background as a portrait painter and muralist as well as an illustrator. The depth of the image is reinforced by her use of the dropped shadow. *November 1931.*

Harvey Nichols

Fortnum & Mason

Marshall & Snelgrove

The dull and shiny side of flesh satin in a princess slip with knickers in satin and chiffon.

Pretty enough for parties: shell pink georgette nightgown, with net ruffles and satin ribbon sash.

Chiffon in shell pink with grouped pleats and a tied waist. Knickers to match.

Debenham & Freebody

A connection, though slender, between brassière and knickers of peach satin and wine racine lace.

Walpoles

A triple alliance: heavy écru lace with black chiffon and cobwebby black lace.

Walpoles

Nightie-pyjama in soft white satin with deep yoke and frills of écru lace. Tie at back.

Left: Simple, almost cartoon-like pen-and-ink sketches depicting lingerie available from various London department stores. The garments evidence the popularity of the bias cut and the simple lines of the daywear of the period. *February 1933.*

Above: Flowing, expressive strokes convey the energy of movement in these monochrome line-and-wash drawings by Anna Zinkeisen. The rounded forms of the figures resonate with the work of Fernand Leger. *November 1931.*

Left: Designers generally chose to depict a group of figures on a single page in odd numbers. Malaga Grenet illustrates three evening dresses by American designer Mainbocher that evidence the era's preoccupation with stylish backless eveningwear and the bias cut. *July 1933.*

Right: Innovative pattern cutting and sharp tailoring were a feature of 1930s fashion: even beachwear was cut with the finesse of eveningwear. Illustrator Eric Fraser casts dark shadows on the figures, emphasizing the sunlit scene. *July 1934.*

TWO SHILLINGS NETT

HARPER'S BAZAAR

INCORPORATING "VANITY FAIR"

February, 1933

SPRING
FABRICS
NUMBER

Left: The angle of this highly dynamic figure forms a diagonal slash of vibrant colour softened by the texture of the powdered snow, drawing the eye to the magazine's title. *February 1933.*

Right: The covers of *Harper's Bazaar* are generally weighted towards the bottom right-hand corner, the image indicating the title above, as here in this work by Leon Bénigni. The treatment of the water in the background implies the speed and movement inherent in the Art Deco period. *July 1932.*

TWO SHILLINGS NETT

HARPER'S BAZAAR

INCORPORATING "VANITY FAIR"

JULY · 1932

HOLIDAY
FASHIONS

Above and right: The suntan is rendered desirable in these drawings by Eric Fraser. None of these models are static; all are adjusting their dress or posing, recreating a vivid tableau. Note, however, the lack of background, which gives the scene an unrealistic studio-based quality. *July 1933.*

Following page: Sportswear tended towards androgyny; the similarity of the male and female silhouette can be seen in the crisp tailoring, the small, neat head, and even the espadrilles. The design of the image is mirrored from the centre, with three figures facing each other across the page. The composition is held together by the use of the central motif, in this case the umbrella. *August 1933.*

Left and right: Illustrator, graphic artist, posterist, fashion designer, ballet and theatre set and costume designer Charles Martin (1884–1934) contributed to the French fashion journals *Gazette du Bon Ton*, *Modes et Manieres d'Aujourd'hui*, *Journal Des Dames et Des Modes*, and *Vogue*. Here he describes the age of leisure and the country house party. A nocturnal scene is made vivacious by the firework scene and the front-lit gowns. *August 1933.*

Left: Skiing was a popular sport with the leisured classes, providing plenty of inspiration for fashion illustration. Anna Zinkeisen portrays an array of knitted fashions by, from left: Robert Douglas, Jaeger, Henri & Mawdsley, Leathercraft and Fortnum & Mason. The depiction of the snow provides a white background allowing the colour to add a three-dimensional depth. *December 1933.*

Left: Neckline detail was an important element of 1930s fashion design, here given emphasis with blocks of deep Fauve-inspired colours forming the fur-trimmed collar and taffeta bow. The impact of the image lies in the equal distribution of colour and neutral background and the cropped figures. *April 1933.*

Right: Conveying the mood of American figurative painter Edward Hopper, the illustrator Carolyn Edmundson has placed the figures in the context of a South American landscape, reflecting the flamenco influence of the frilled, floor-length dresses. *February 1934.*

Right and far right:
Following photographic
convention, Charles
Martin renders
these garments with
quick detailing against
a soft focus background.
April 1934.

Shadows Before

Don Juan Designs

by OLIVER MESSEL

Above: Oliver Messel (1904–1978) was the leading British stage designer of the mid-20th century. His theatrical background is evident in these sketches, which depict the illusion rather than the reality of garments. His gift of imaginative pastiche extends to the figures, and their theatrical poses. *July 1934.*

Right: Utilizing quick, spontaneous strokes of white chalk on a black background, Marcel Vertès animates the female form. By inverting the colours the image immediately gains dramatic effect. *March 1934.*

Left and right:
Deliberately unfinished
drawings by Charles
Martin lends a casual,
spontaneous air to the
background of large-scale
trellis and flowers,
redolent of Art Deco.
The black patterning
of the prints provides
a stark contrast to the
softly shaded pencil
drawings of the white
figures. *August 1934.*

YRANDE   YRANDE   MOLYNEUX

Left and right: In contrast to the tailored functionality of daywear in the 1930s, evening dresses were influenced by the glamorous stars of the Hollywood screen. The use of black with the pink wash of the background in this pen-and-ink illustration by American-born Helen Jameson Hall conveys the sophisticated elegance of the era. *September 1934.*

Above: Conveyed in watercolour inks and brushstrokes, the hats are the focus of these two illustrations by Christian Berard. The French artist and designer (1902–1949), also known as Bébé, adopts the convention of the mirror to show the back view. *November 1934.*

Left: An insouciant pose captured by Christian Berard in dashes of swift, expressive dry brushstrokes and watercolour inks. *October 1934.*

Right: Spanish painter and printmaker Pedro Pruna (1904–1977) describes the theatricality of bias-cut tartan with energetic, casual brushstrokes of complementary colours. *October 1934.*

Above and right: The etiolated bodies and hard, sinuous forms of the dresses are depicted with a single brushstroke in these two illustrations by Christian Berard. The neutral uncluttered background throws into relief the intense complementary colours of the garments, which are accessorized with a single vase of flowers. *December 1934.*

Far right: The figures form an overall pattern, interspersed by colour blocks of garments in this illustration by A.K. Zinkeisen. The portrayal of the hair is an Art Deco speed motif, implying in this case a turbulent breeze. The garments are finely detailed in contrast to the mere indication of the limbs. *June 1935.*

Left: Stylized, solid blocks of colour drawn by Reynaldo Luza emphasize the broad-shouldered, narrow-hipped silhouette of the era. The cropped figure in the corner draws the eye to the two main protagonists on the page and amplifies the details of the garments. *April 1936.*

Right: A portrait of French couturier Nina Ricci (1883–1970), founder of the eponymous house in 1932. Although executed in the 1930s, the hairstyle, the gigot sleeves of the dress and the opulent padded and quilted chair are more redolent of the earlier decades of the 20th century. *February 1936.*

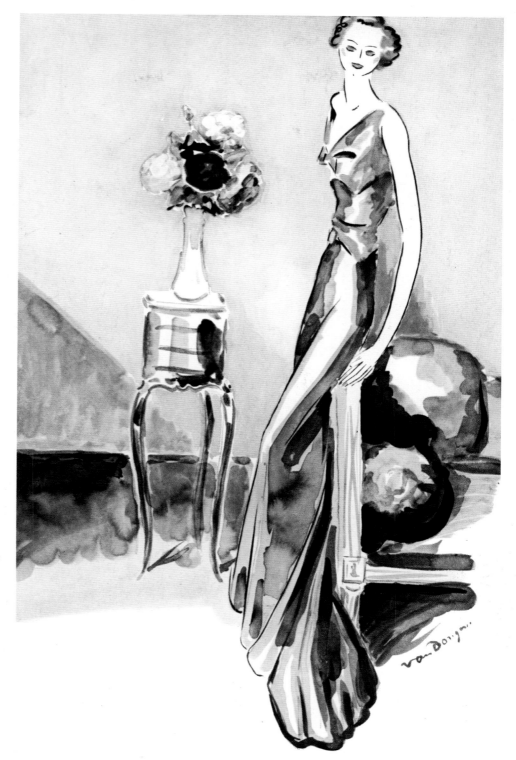

Left: A mysterious landscape and dramatic floor-length cloak are conveyed through the watercolour technique of aquarelle. The nightscape is given depth by the siting of the figure in the foreground and the backlit horizon. *July 1935.*

Right: Dutch-born Kees van Dongen (1877–1968) participated in the *Salon d'Automne* of 1905, which established Fauvism as a new movement in modern art. His distinctive style and sumptuous colour palette is evidenced here in his illustration of a dress in lamé by Mainbocher. *September 1935.*

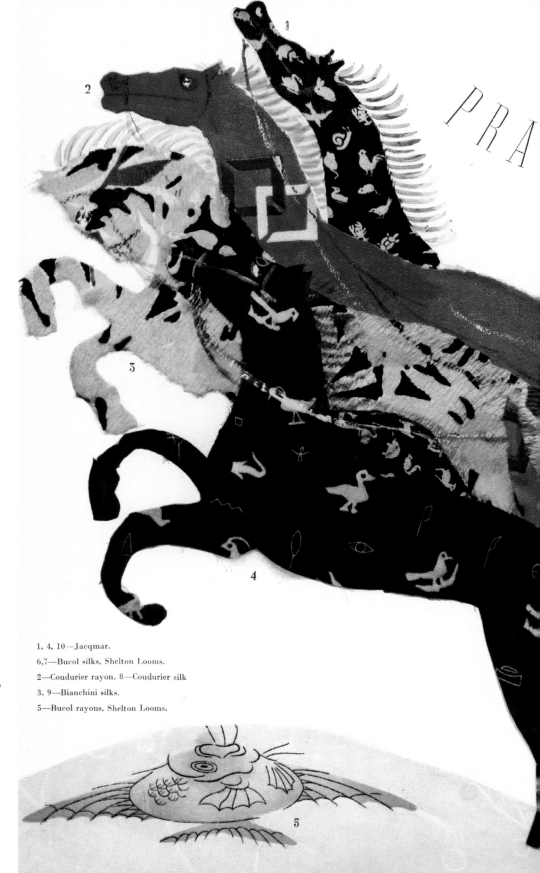

PRA

1, 4, 10—Jacqmar.

6, 7—Bucol silks, Shelton Looms.

2—Coudurier rayon. 8—Coudurier silk

3, 9—Bianchini silks.

5—Bucol rayons, Shelton Looms.

Right: Referencing Sandro Botticelli's *Birth of Venus* (c.1485) the young girl charioteer reins in her horses, which are decorated in various printed and patterned headscarves. *March 1936.*

E OF SPRING

Left and right: Muted colours and draped and tailored elegance are evident in these evening gowns illustrated by Laza. The depiction of the figures, posed in front of a faux-collaged background, show how the stylized format of the 1930s is evolving towards a more realistic approach to fashion illustration in the coming decade. *July 1936.*

Following page: A Surrealist Dalí-inspired dreamscape of coloured chalks on a dark background provides the perfect foil for Elsa Schiaparelli's 'newspaper bonnets'. The iconoclastic designer was renowned for her imaginative and innovative use of materials. *June 1935.*

Left and right: Recalling the photographer Man Ray's 'Rayograms' these images from soft-focus negatives are colour retouched by hand, giving an ethereal quality to the figures. *March 1937.*

Left: Named after the brightest star in the constellation Lyra, the Guerlain perfume Vega provides the illustrator Darcy with the stellar motif behind the model's head. The design also resonates with America's symbol of hope and freedom, the Statue of Liberty. *May 1937.*

Right: This sugar-pink toque is rendered in lively, Dufy-esque, dashing lines and expressive flourishes by Marcel Vertès. *June 1938.*

Left and below: The crayon sketch below by French painter, poet and film maker Jean Cocteau (1889–1963) shows his complete authority of line. The figure on the left is more crudely executed, but contains all the elements associated with French couturier Coco Chanel; the understated skirt and blouse, the oversize pearls and black bob secured with a ribbon bow. *June 1937.*

Right: Artists and fashion designers shared the same creative milieu in pre-war Europe and New York, interchanging ideas and working outside the conventional boundaries of each other discipline. Here, Jean Cocteau evidences his mastery of line and contour. *May 1936.*

Far right: The dramatic and mysterious associations of this figure reference the wicked step-mother in Walt Disney's film *Snow White and the Seven Dwarfs* (1937). *June 1937.*

Above: Garments designed by French couturier Coco Chanel provide her friend and colleague Jean Cocteau the opportunity to present two decadent caryatid figures. The figure on the left shows a meticulous rendering of his own print design. *June 1939.*

Right: A new silhouette began to emerge at the end of the decade. Inspired by the work of 19th-century painter Franz Xavier Winterhalter, designers such as Edward Molyneux attempted to introduce the hourglass figure. The full skirt and draped bodice is executed in gouache, utilizing dry brushwork to describe the folds of cloth. *April 1938.*

Left: Evident in this illustration is a move away from the stylization of face and form that typified 1930s illustration techniques, towards a more modern and realistic representation. The classic rendering of drapery and the model's expressive features provide an indication of the increasing importance in fashion illustration of drawing from life. *May 1938.*

Right: A Victorian-inspired dress reflects a silhouette in transition from the liquid falls of the full skirt of the late 1930s to the square-shouldered tailoring of the 1940s. Designed by British dressmaker Norman Hartnell, the garment is rendered in gouache. *September 1937.*

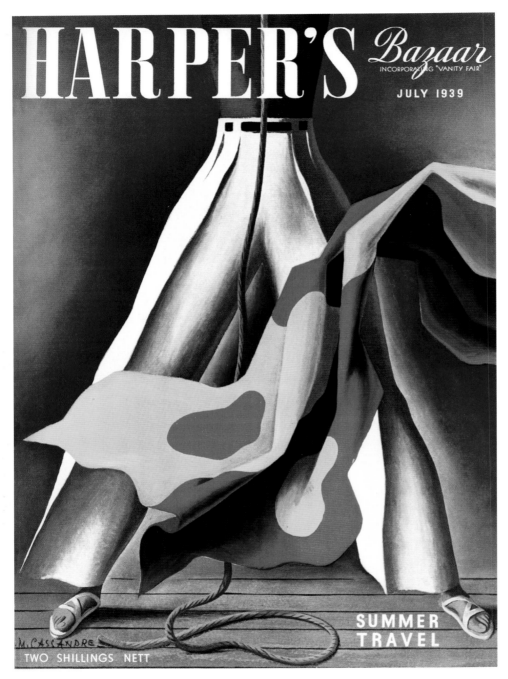

HARPER'S *Bazaar*
INCORPORATING "VANITY FAIR"

JULY 1939

SUMMER
TRAVEL

TWO SHILLINGS NETT

Left: Born in the Ukraine to French parents, the work of illustrator A.M. Cassandre, (1901–1968) exemplified Art Deco images and typefaces. He was renowned for his travel posters, particularly those for the SS *Normandie* Cruise line and the Nord express. In this design he references the power of Russian Constructivism and the work of Kazimir Malevich. *July 1939.*

Right: Eschewing a more conventional approach to selling cosmetics, this illustration by Darcy for Guerlain lipstick suggests a dreamy sensual state of bliss engendered by the application of red lipstick. *September 1937.*

GUERLAIN

THE LIPSTICK OF YOUR DREAMS

1940s

Previous page: The graphic immediacy of the bold block of red and the linear execution of the coat imply an inherent, sophisticated glamour to this simple ensemble. *March 1949.*

Above: During the 1940s, fashion illustration moved away from the stylization of the Art Deco period and began to offer a more realistic representation of the human figure. In addition, the figures were often placed within a context, providing both a narrative, as here, which was also a vehicle to convey the fashions of the day. *March 1941.*

Right: This June bride wears a Renaissance Juliet-inspired wedding dress rendered in watercolour against an *ombréd* background. *June 1940.*

HARPER'S

June *Bazaar*

INCORPORATING "VANITY FAIR"

Brides and Beauty
TWO SHILLINGS NETT

HARPER'S

May

Bazaar

INCORPORATING "VANITY FAIR"

FENRION

Three Shillings

Left: Designers were given total licence to incorporate the logo of *Harper's Bazaar* magazine into the design of the cover. Here, illustrator Frederic Henri Kay Henrion, (1914–1990) has angled the letters of the title to reflect the wind-blown uniforms on the patriotic maypole. German-born Henrion emigrated to England in 1939, adopting British nationality in 1946. *May 1942.*

Right: American swimsuit manufacturer Jantzen is still recognized by the insignia of the diving girl, one of the oldest of fashion brand icons. It first appeared in advertisements for the company in the 1920s. The logo was sewn or embroidered onto Jantzen swimsuits from 1923, at the same time as the tagline appeared 'the suit that changed bathing to swimming'. Swimsuits became more streamlined according to technical advances and the more relaxed dress codes of the 1930s, allowing for the air-brushed perfection of near-naked bodies. *June 1940.*

"SKIP THE FLATTERY, DARLING MY JANTZEN TAKES CARE OF THAT"

Irresistible as ever, swim suits by Jantzen once again put temptation in your way. With gorgeous colours and lovely figure-moulding fabrics, many with Lastex yarn knitted-in, Jantzen stylists have worked summer magic. Jantzen tailoring adds the final touch to a range of inspiring brilliance.

Shown here, Mademoiselle 29/6, and Half-Hitch Trunks 13/9

Jantzen

GREAT WEST ROAD, BRENTFORD, MIDDLESEX

SWIM SUITS & LEISURE WEAR

COME OUT TO PLAY IN JANTZEN

Jantzen Sports Wear for women is just one inspiration after another. See and be charmed by playsuits, slacks, shorts, jumpers, tunics, shirts, and a host...

Above and left: The Queen's dressmaker (the term couturier refers only to French designers) Norman Hartnell was involved in a war-time export drive to sell British fashion to South America. The resulting designs were incorporated into his London collections, and worn by Queen Elizabeth II. *March 1941.*

Right: This all-over cover design by Henrion had added drama and impact from the reversed-out font of the title and the disciplined organization of the two heads and the beautifully depicted glove. The treatment of the face owes something to the style of the Russian artist Marc Chagall. *September 1942.*

HARPER'S BAZAAR

INCORPORATING "VANITY FAIR"

SEPTEMBER

PRICE THREE SHILLINGS

HENRION

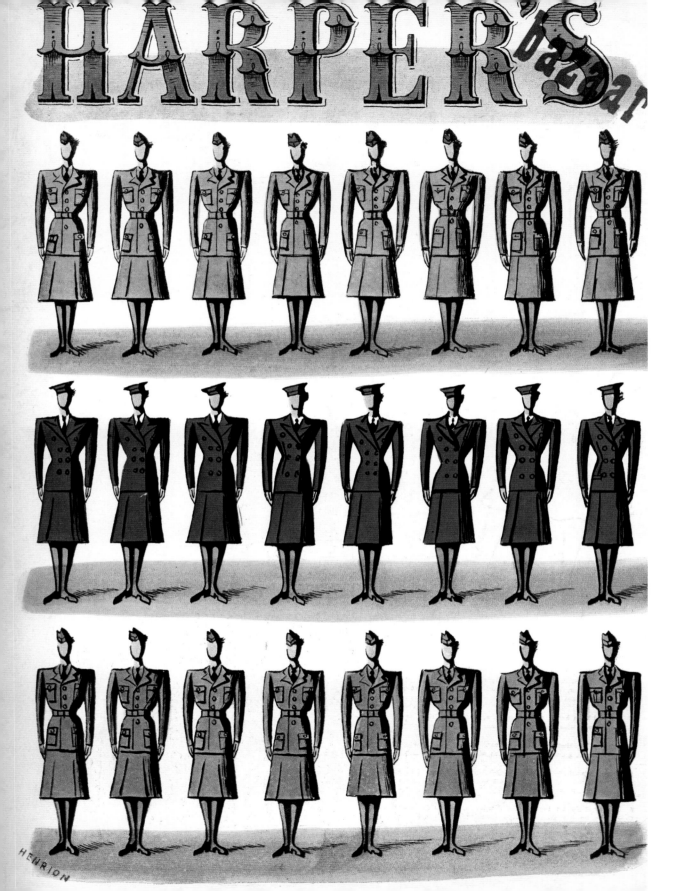

HENRION

Left: During World War II Henrion designed posters for the British Ministry of Information, which helped establish his international reputation. This cover describes the uniform of the three services — army, navy and air force — in three rhythmic stripes. *June 1942.*

Right: The onset of World War II was to delay the attempt by couturiers, including Charles Worth, to recrinolinize the female form. This darkly gothic evening dress delineated in a broad, even stroke, also references the gigot sleeve of the 19th century. *September 1940.*

Left: Quick, monochrome sketches of maternity wear showing little more than detail. They were probably drawn in-house, rather than by a professional illustrator. *September 1942.*

Right: An economy of line and brushstroke describes the square-shouldered silhouette that emerged during the war years, the severity of which is here offset by the frivolous hat. *August 1942.*

Above and left: Speedily executed pen-and-wash sketches. The finesse lies in the rendering of a variety of furs, from sheepskin to wolf, with a minimum of brushstrokes. *November 1942.*

Right: 'Digging for Victory'. Illustrated by T.W. (Tage Werner), the figure and vegetable subject matter is portrayed in the lively, expressionistic style of Henri Matisse. *June 1943.*

Following page: During war-time, Britain's Board of Trade imposed limitations on the number of colours to be used in printed fabrics. Here the designs are collaged together by T.W. in a faux flowerbed against a background of industrious gardeners wearing 'utility' clothes. *April 1943.*

Spring Cottons and Rayons

Left: Evidence of the influence of Surrealist painter Salvador Dali shows in this illustration by Henrion. The tumbling lowercase letters of the title echo the disconcerting disruption of the drooping carnation and the profiled head draped in a scarf which depicts emblems of the armed forces. *May 1943.*

Right and below: The colouration of the illustration by T.W. – ruby reds, golds and emeralds – reinforce the notion of buried treasure in reinvented garments during a period of make-do-and-mend and recycling. *February 1943.*

Following page: Rendering the mundane special, Henrion provides evidence of the influence of the Surrealist movement on fashion illustration in his depiction of printed fabrics caught among the branches of trees, some of which have taken on the form of mannequins. *June 1943.*

JAEGER

The best in Utility

Left: British mass-market manufacturer Jaeger here offers their version of the 'utility' suit. The Board of Trade had rules and regulations on the design of women's clothes. The 'utility scheme' was a set of approved garments designed by several prominent names including Hardy Amies and Norman Hartnell. These low-cost, democratic garments gave women who could never normally afford *haute couture* a chance to experience the cut of well-designed garments. *February 1944.*

Right: A *croquis* (from the French word 'sketch') is a quick drawing of a 'live' model, holding the pose for a limited time for the artist to render an overall impression of the garments, as here in this monochrome brush-and-ink drawing by T.W. *September 1943.*

Left: Resonant of Soviet Heroic Realism, this figure is drawn from below, providing a monumental quality to the pose. The tail feathers of the pheasant and the rifle form a diagonal movement across the page, adding emphasis to the image. *February 1944.*

Above and right: The squared-off shoulders, narrow skirt and wide lapels of the high-fastening collar in this tweed coat reflect the influence of military uniform on civilian dress. The coat, cleverly camouflaged against the fabric background, is simply described in a confident brush-and-ink line. *February 1944.*

HARPER'S

April   Bazaar

TW.

THREE SHILLINGS

Left: Fauve colours and technique are deployed BY T.W. in the feathered hat and scarf, leaving the face and features to blend in with the light brown background. *April 1944.*

Right: A gouache rendering of a tailored coat and dress, the complementary colours darkened down to provide a sombre Hopper-esque image emphasized by the thunderous colour of the background. *March 1944.*

Corduroy

Yesterday
vaguely drab
To-day – a
kaleidoscope
of colour

A Deréta coat with
rounded revers and
roomy patch pockets.
At Marshall & Snelgrove,
Leeds.

Well-tailored Deréta suit-
slim panelled skirt,
welted slanting pockets
in jacket
At Bourne & Hollingsworth

Below: Collarless coat, the fitting line at centre back
...ding in a pleat. Deréta at Bourne & Hollingsworth
...Worn over a Dorville
...shirtwaist dress.

Inset belt outlines
...o pockets and fastens
at back
...t Bon Marché
Liverpool

Below: A high
fastening Dorville suit
with interesting vertical
breast pockets. Skirt
is straight with centre
back and front pleats.
At Harrods

T.W.

HARPER'S

June   *Bazaar*

THREE SHILLINGS

Previous page: War-time fashion in hard-wearing corduroy. The ribbed texture of the fabric is described by T.W. in a loose watercolour wash overlaid with light brushstrokes. The four figures point in the same direction across the double spread; together with the angled background wash this lends a sense of urgent activity. *March 1944.*

Left: A more light-hearted approach is becoming evident as the war draws to a close in this cover design by T.W. Although the coat still retains a military cut, the rose-patterned snood and dress are rendered in the lively expressionistic style of Matisse and Dufy. *June 1944.*

Right: Eveningwear tended to retain the glamour of the pre-war years, as seen in this Matisse-like treatment by T.W., with the upright figure at the forefront of the picture and the reclining figure on the sofa brought to life by rapid impressionistic brushstrokes. *May 1944.*

Above: The fabric manufacturer Jacqmar was known for producing propaganda prints during the war years. In this illustration by T.W., the model flies the flag with this patriotic head square. *June 1944.*

Above: Accessories achieved a new importance in times of clothes rationing, being an affordable and accessible way to ring the changes in a war-time wardrobe. The headscarf became a versatile alternative to the hat, as seen in these drawings by T.W. *June 1944.*

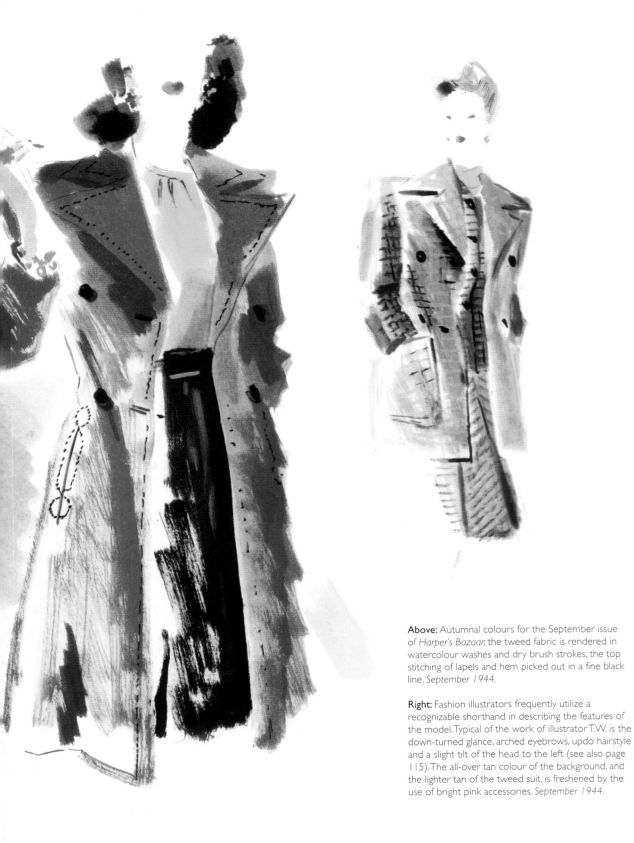

Above: Autumnal colours for the September issue of *Harper's Bazaar*, the tweed fabric is rendered in watercolour washes and dry brush strokes, the top stitching of lapels and hem picked out in a fine black line. *September 1944.*

Right: Fashion illustrators frequently utilize a recognizable shorthand in describing the features of the model. Typical of the work of illustrator T.W. is the down-turned glance, arched eyebrows, updo hairstyle and a slight tilt of the head to the left (see also page 115). The all-over tan colour of the background, and the lighter tan of the tweed suit, is freshened by the use of bright pink accessories. *September 1944.*

HARPER'S

Bazaar

Jan–Feb 1945

THREE SHILLINGS

Left and below centre: Clothes rationing in Britain did not come to an end until 1949, so these Parisian garments illustrated by Bosc in 1945 with their full skirts and big patch pockets could only be admired by the readers of the magazine. *August 1945.*

Below right: The influence of Dior's New Look can be seen in this summer cotton dress by British manufacturer Horrockses, a major cotton manufacturing firm founded in Lancashire in the 18th century. The Horrockses cotton dress, usually full-skirted, was a popular summer staple for British women. *January 1949.*

Left: Cheerfully facing the future, this cover illustration utilizes the diagonal slant of the image to provide movement across the page and indicate the title. The fur of the hood is described by excising the top layer of paint and drawing out the brushstrokes into the dark background. *February 1945.*

Left: Fabric manufacturer Moygashel produced a range of linen-mix fabrics in a wide variety of colours, here illustrated in a decorative display of parachutes, a familiar sight from the newsreels of the invasion of Europe. *November 1944.*

Right: The return to domesticity and the importance of a stable family life in contrast to the upheaval of the war years is reflected in this illustration for matching mother-and-children camel coats in the advertisement for British company Jaeger. *December 1944.*

Right: The typical pose of tilted head and downward glance is recognizably the work of T.W. The use of blocks of two complementary colours – red and green – provide a dramatic cover emphasized by the diagonal brush marks of the solid background. *November 1944.*

Above left: Celebrating sailors throwing their caps in the air feature on this single-colour print, made up into a shirtwaister dress with padded shoulders and front pockets. *May 1945.*

Above centre: A three-piece summer suit by French illustrator Jacques Demachy. A sense of sun-worshipping tourism is evoked by the dark tan wash and straw hat. *July 1949.*

Right: The artist's rendition of the dress adds green to the original two-colour swatch of the fabric. Hats were designed to add femininity to an outfit to offset the masculine silhouette of the clothes. *May 1945.*

HARPER'S

November

Bazaar

THREE SHILLINGS

Left: An almost photographic representation of Hollywood glamour, where the figure is framed by the blackground. The illustration features a draped front dress, providing an example of the fluid qualities of Courtaulds rayon. *May 1945.*

Right: The models pose in traditional hand-on-hip style to display the embellished tops beneath the jackets. The perfunctory representation of the model's features focuses all the attention on the garments. *November 1944.*

Left: This advertisement for 'foundation' garments by Demachy discreetly indicates only the suggestion of a body beneath the clothes. The arms are reaching upwards to pull on a filmsy outer garment, represented by a few painterly brush marks excised from the dark ground. *October 1949.*

Right: Looking towards the future with a new spirit of optimism is heralded in this cover design by Bosc. The sketchy, brightly coloured print design and rendering of the figure is in the style of French painter Raoul Dufy (1877–1953). *June 1945.*

Left: The chair and folds of the dress are rendered in impasto – with a salute to Oskar Kokoschka – by illustrator Victor. This contrasts with the finely delineated and smooth, even-toned legs of the model and the black shoes, which are the subject of the advertisement. *February 1949.*

Above: Two *croquis* by Jacques Demachy, which display the longer-length, defined waist and softer shoulder indicating the emergence of the hourglass figure that was typical of the coming decade. *February 1949.*

Right: The fluid folds of this draped and ruched evening dress in wool jersey by Mary Black are rendered in brush and ink by Demachy. *February 1949.*

Norman Hartnell designs fairy-tale
evening dresses.
Left, peacock net picture
dress with sequin roses. Right, amber
slipper satin with china blue beads.

Above: The crinoline returns, in this richly embroidered design by the Queen's dressmaker Norman Hartnell. These graphite drawings with the figure in half-shadow, render a sombre majesty to the subject matter, creating an evocation of the chiaroscuro in paintings of dancers by Edgar Degas. *March 1949.*

Right: Some illustrators rooted their work in realism rather than stylization and employed models to wear the garments that they were commissioned to document. Consequently the poses used could be better adapted to dramatize the more significant aspects of the designs – such as the front-opening skirt or the gathered swing-back of the jacket. The three poses in this tableau, with the garments and accessories defined in white gouache, are held together by a loose rectangle of tan-toned colour wash. *July 1949.*

HARPER'S

Bazaar

London Fashions

Tweeds

Furs

September · 1949

Below: The end of rationing resulted in a widespread acceptance of the archetypal silhouette of the era. Dolman sleeves caught into a tight waist that flares into a full, gathered or pleated calf-length skirt, the fullness of the skirt emphasized by the large patch pockets with flaps. *August 1949.*

Left: The cover title of *Harper's Bazaar* is no longer incorporated into the design; the font now remains the same throughout every issue. The figure forms the 'golden triangle' of design, the apex being the brightly described red hat. *September 1949.*

Above left: A robust drawing from life underpins the immediacy of this rapid sketch in colour washes, detailed with impressionistic, flicked brush lines. *June 1949.*

Above centre: Paired with a drop-shouldered, swing-backed jacket, the slim tubular skirt that fell below the knee was one of the two quintessential silhouettes offered by Parisian couturier Christian Dior, the other being the swirling, full, gathered or pleated calf-length skirt of the Corolle line, dubbed the New Look by journalists. *December 1949.*

1950s

HARPER'S

Bazaar

February 1950

Building Your Spring Wardrobe

Previous page: The lack of shaded drape and the mechanical repetition of the floral motif suggest a jacquard woven brocade, rather than a lighter, printed fabric. *January 1955.*

Left: The arrangement of beads and braids is laid flat on the paper and photographed in this cover from February 1950; the casual spontaneity and playfulness of this exercise in collage is implied by the curl of paper. *February 1950.*

Right: Nylon replaced silk and cotton stockings and the invention of fully fashioned, 12-denier stockings rendered hosiery almost invisible, except for the seam up the back of the leg. Kayser Bondor became a household name, sustained by advertising, which here borrows the glamour of Cyd Charisse and the hyper-realism of the air-brushed pin-up. *August 1950.*

KAYSER BONDOR

for sheer beauty in full fashioned stockings

Spring challenge...

Left: Freelance designer and illustrator Alastair Michie (1921–1970) went on to become a renowned painter and sculptor in the early 1960s. This lively pose is both modern and youthful, the print of the skirt is described with a light hand, in contrast to the solid colour of the sweater. *April 1950.*

Right: This illustration is distinguished by the painstakingly rendered check of the tweed coat surrounded by the artfully arranged nosegays of flowers. *March 1950.*

Simpson
PICCADILLY

Above: Conveying a sophisticated evening urbanity, this narrative depicts the importance of ladylike decorum and attention to grooming, both of which were prerequisites of the 1950s woman – personified by Anna Neagle in the 'London films' of *Springtime in Park Lane* (1948) and *Maytime in Mayfair* (1949). *October 1950.*

Right: Classic country tweeds illustrated with great economy by Demachy in pen and watercolour. Using an elevated horizon and the simple device of 'retreating colour' – that is, with colder hues in the distance – the illustrator opens the sense of a vast panorama with a minimum of brushstrokes. *January 1951.*

Below: Mix 'n' match'
was a phenomenon of
the American sportswear
designers such as Claire
McCardell and Hattie
Carnegie. In this
illustration, the wardrobe
includes tailored shorts,
a halter-necked, fitted
blouse, a short wrap skirt,
a swimsuit and a dirndl
skirt. The white pique
duster coat was designed
to cover the ensemble
beneath. *June 1950.*

Left and right: During the 1950s, Paris dictated fashionable style and *haute couture* reached its apotheosis with the work of Pierre Balmain, Cristóbel Balenciaga, Christian Dior and Jaques Fath. *September 1950*.

Right: In the era of the Hollywood musicals, such as *Summer Stock* (1950) and *A Star is Born* (1954), the illustrator dramatizes the copy line, 'Step out in Wolsey nylons', by uplighting the theatrically articulated figure and implying a red velvet curtain call with a single broad brushstroke of watercolour. *June 1953.*

BY APPOINTMENT
HOSIERY MANUFACTURERS
TO THE LATE KING GEORGE VI

Step out in

Wolsey

nylons

Right: With the Oscar-winning arrival of Audrey Hepburn in *Roman Holiday* (1953) and in the title role in *Sabrina* (1954), the unsmiling mannequin of the early 1950s began to give way to a friendlier, more gamine and wide-eyed model, particularly in advertising with the emergence of the youth market as a new consumer. *February 1955.*

Left: Hatching – a system of building up the tones and shadows of a drawing by applying the pencil, chalk or paint in a series of lines – is deployed here to describe a series of garments and accessories of delicate and differing textures. *August 1952.*

Right: The cropped figure is rendered more dramatic by the depth of shadow to the left of the figure. The fashion illustrations of the era reflected the poses of the photographic models such as Suzy Parker; poised with hips thrust forward, unsmiling and with a degree of hauteur. *March 1950.*

dresses
and suits
in

FABRICS
Lombardi

Left: Demachy uses gouache for a strong background of colour and foliar texture to dramatize the mannered figure in this illustrated advertisement for Lombardi Fabrics. The slinky silhouette of the belted, button-through dress is accessorized in great detail – offset by the 'has everything' haughtiness of the head. *November 1955.*

Right: Rattan, rubber plant and giant straw hat, together with the dark tan of the figure, all evoke the topical exoticism of the tropical Pacific. Films such as *From Here to Eternity* (1953) held sway in the common imagination and this sultry treatment by Demachy of an asymmetrically collared sheath dress exploits this genre. *July 1953.*

flawlessly lovely

Twin-set BY Wolsey

Left: A wardrobe staple of the era, associated with classic good taste and a string of pearls, the twinset is illustrated here to appeal to a more youthful market. The ingénue, Hepburn look-alike model wears a 'poodle' hair cut. The style of heavy line and colour fill has faint and sanitized echoes of Henri Matisse and Max Beckmann. *March 1955.*

Right: Audrey Hepburn appeared with the chic accessory of a European poodle both in the film *Sabrina* (1954) and as a dog owner in real life. Here Demachy uses both Hepburn and poodle references to indicate the light-hearted but sophisticated polish of the traveller. *March 1955.*

dresses
and suits
in

FABRICS

Lombardi

Fabrics Lombardi Ltd., Abbey Park Road,
Leicester. Phone 22812.

HARPER'S

Bazaa

International Collection

September 195

Left: Jane Bixby (born 1926) trained at the American Academy of Art, Chicago, and Cooper Union, New York. Some fashion illustration clients include Marshall Field & Co. and Saks Fifth Ave. She also produced editorial illustration for *Harper's Bazaar*, covering the fashion collections in Italy and Paris. The reversed-out *Harper's* title in the orange background keeps the emphasis squarely on the bold form of the sculptured head. *September 1956.*

Right: Elegant *Croquis* describe the *haute couture* collections of Elsa Schiaparelli and Robert Piguet, the figures in typical mannequin poses. The simplicity of media disguises the elegance of the representational skill invested in these painted sketches, where density and handle of material is implied solely from the weight of line and opacity of paint deployed. *March 1951.*

Left and right: During the 1950s spectacles became an accessory, subject to fashionable trends, as seen here illustrated by A.G. Bouret. The exaggerated, horn-rimmed eyewear shared the same inspiration as the American finned automobile or the new supersonic jet aircraft. The crisp, hard-edged graphic treatment echoes this era of positivism. *May 1955.*

Below and right: Creating an ambience of Hepburn gamine, the three components of this illustration by A.G. Bouret are held together by the tight two-colour palette. *May 1955.*

Far right: Using wash and line in just two colours, A.G. Bouret collects disparate items into a flowing group. The line of the upper of the shoe leads to the canopy of the umbrella, which fulfils an invisible circuit by skirting the curved hem of the dress before inflecting to the arc of the bag handle and reflecting both the crook of the umbrella handgrip and the arch of the heel. *May 1955.*

Cashmere time...

Above: By cropping the two figures at hip height with an arbitrary table line of silhouetted goblets, Demachy pushes the focus upon the Pringle knitwear that is the subject of this advertisement by Simpson of Piccadilly. The animated curiosity implied by the lowered lids, elevated chins and arched eyebrows of the figures subliminally suggests heightened levels of discernment. *October 1955.*

Simpson
PICCADILLY

Sun sorcery...

Sail away to blue horizons via Simpsons in Piccadilly where you can choose beguiling clothes like these to put you in the mood for enchanted idling.

Striped and flower-strewn pinafore dress to prettify many occasions : sunning on the beach; dressed up with a blouse; over its bloomer suit. Concealed buttons go all the way down the front. Striped in pink, cornflower blue, primrose, or pigeon grey. Sizes 10—14. Dress and suit together, £10.15.0.

Tailored nylon dress lightly striped in its own colour, with pin-tucked bodice and skirt stiffened by its taffeta petticoat. Trim collar and cuffed cap-sleeves. Yellow or lilac. Sizes 10—16. 9½ gns.

You can also order through the Simpson Post Order Service.

Simpson
PICCADILLY

Women's Resort Wear—fourth fl

Simpson (Piccadilly) Ltd, London W.1 Regent 20

HARPER'S

October 1951   Bazaar

Full Report from Paris

Three Shillings and Sixpence

Left: In this quirkily intimate portrait cover by Durani, the accessories are illustrated with an elegant graphic economy of painterly line, linking the solitary contrast of carmine lipstick directly to the *Harper's* title. *October 1951.*

Right: British-born Bernard Nevill is more widely recognized as a print designer, being appointed design director of print during the 1960s at London store Liberty and Professor of Textiles at the Royal College of Art. Here he illustrates with gouache and pen a hound's-tooth check coat and matching accessories. *November 1956.*

HARPER'S

Bazaar

September 1957

Three Shillings & Sixpence

Collections

Paris

London   Italy

Left: The drawn illustration and some fragments of text are boxed in cut-out shapes. The abstract design, focuses the eye on the blue cut-out form of the tall cloche hat which is delineated, together with the profile head, with bold brushstrokes. *September 1957.*

Right: The mannered elegance of this silhouette suggests the balletic stance of stars such as Cyd Charisse, the pose treated here with the graphic theatricality of Henri de Toulouse-Lautrec. *February 1950.*

Following page: All things angular — elbows, profiles, stiletto heels and colour block cutouts — signify an enduring theme in 1950s design. This illustration by Jane Bixby is held in unison by the balance of positive and negative form and by the painterly treatment of the printed dress. *October 1957.*

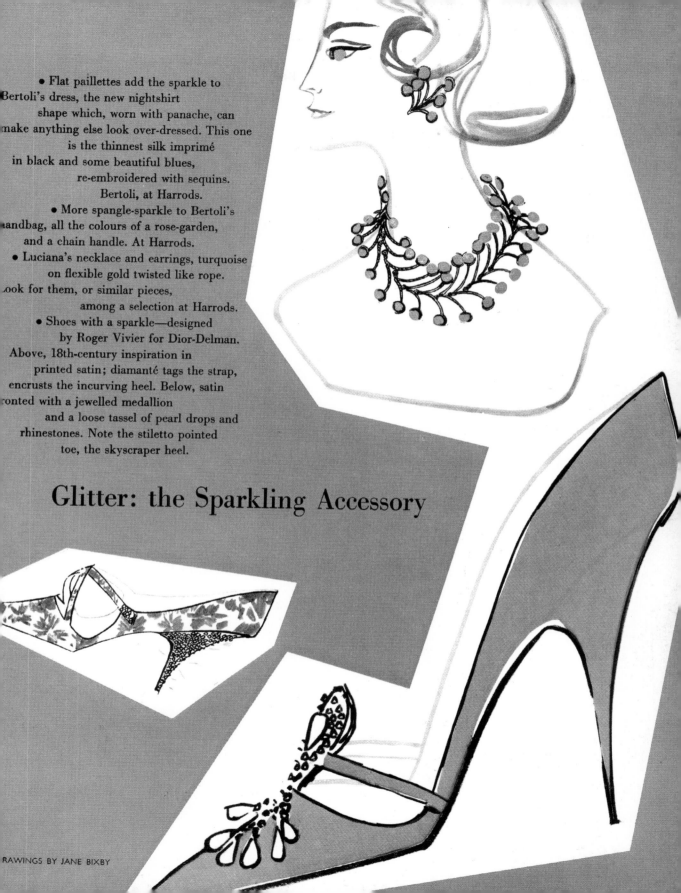

- Flat paillettes add the sparkle to Bertoli's dress, the new nightshirt shape which, worn with panache, can make anything else look over-dressed. This one is the thinnest silk imprimé in black and some beautiful blues, re-embroidered with sequins. Bertoli, at Harrods.

- More spangle-sparkle to Bertoli's handbag, all the colours of a rose-garden, and a chain handle. At Harrods.

- Luciana's necklace and earrings, turquoise on flexible gold twisted like rope. Look for them, or similar pieces, among a selection at Harrods.

- Shoes with a sparkle—designed by Roger Vivier for Dior-Delman. Above, 18th-century inspiration in printed satin; diamanté tags the strap, encrusts the incurving heel. Below, satin fronted with a jewelled medallion and a loose tassel of pearl drops and rhinestones. Note the stiletto pointed toe, the skyscraper heel.

Glitter: the Sparkling Accessory

DRAWINGS BY JANE BIXBY

Left: With the economy and boldness of line of Toulouse-Lautrec or Matisse, here Jane Bixby defines a sculptural daywear outfit with an elegant, cursive brush drawing. *October 1956.*

Right: French painter Paul Gauguin is attributed as the inspiration for this floral print captured in gouache on a dark background. The illustrator has lavished exceptional care in rendering the same print with three distinct levels of opacity: the elasticized satin of the 'swimsheath' is fully opaque, the outer surface of the flyaway voile jacket is less dense (but shows nuances of the other layers of pattern folded beneath), and finally the single layer of the inside of the jacket is discernibly paler than the rest of the garment. The female figure emerges as a simple, but mannered, linear scaffold, rising from the depths of the dark wash background as a black painted line. *March 1959.*

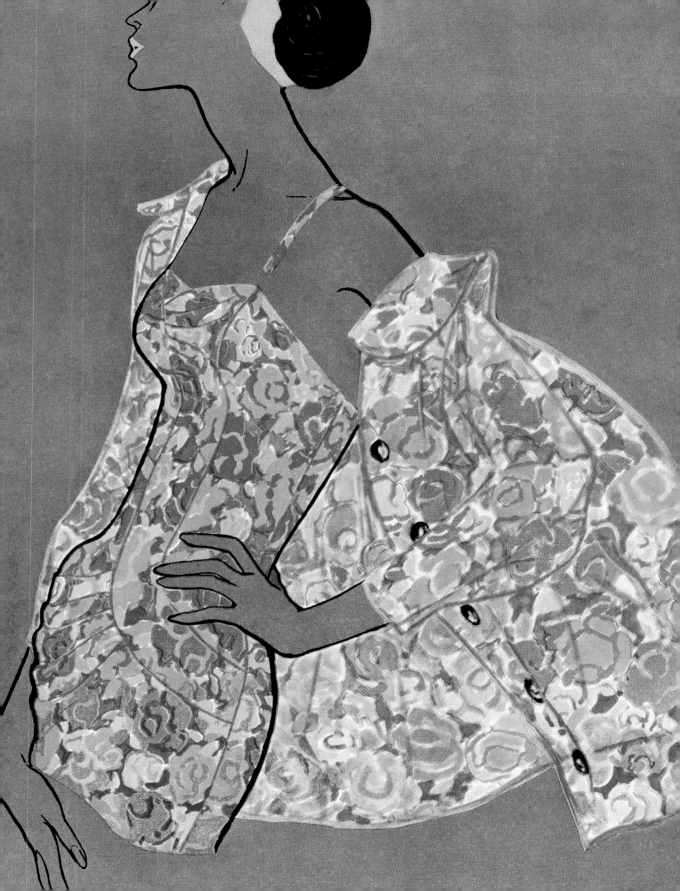

Right and far right: This diptych exploits the repertoire of colour field paintings, as exemplified by the American expressionist Mark Rothko. Hooded sweaters, stretch pants and the dirndl skirt all represent the new freedoms inherent in American sportswear. *December 1957.*

Left and above: The illustrator has used a combination of free brush-and-ink work combined with charcoal to describe the work of celebrated British designers Norman Hartnell, John Cavanagh, Worth and Victor Steibel. Steibel was renowned for his romantic, sculptural evening gowns and was also chairman of the Incorporated Society of London Fashion Designers. *March 1958.*

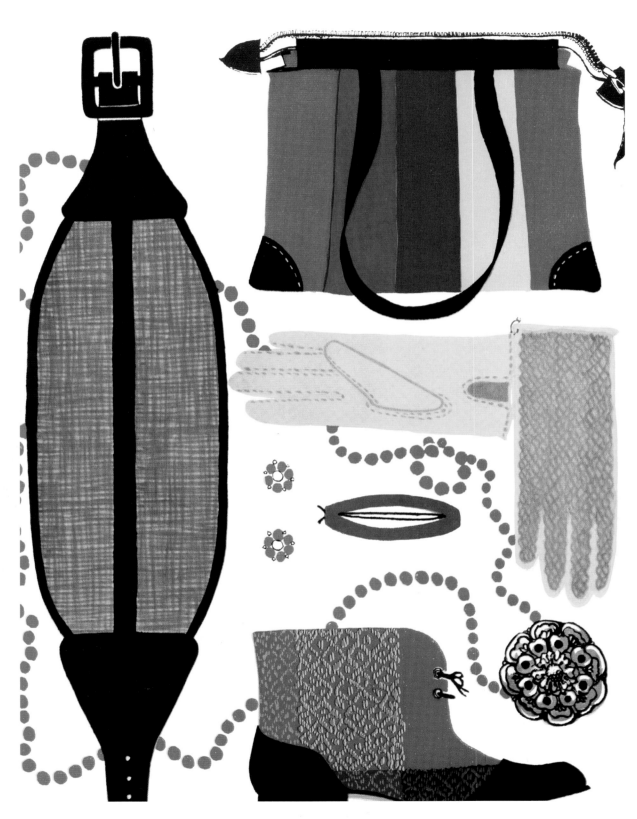

Far left: The contemporary influence of the Pop Art movement can be seen in the flat two-dimensional rendering and the juxtaposition of these accessories within the boundaries of the page. *January 1959.*

Left: A lucid, free-painted study from life. The contrasted background frame creates a forceful composition that communicates both the style of wearing and the documentary detail of the outfit. *August 1958.*

1960s

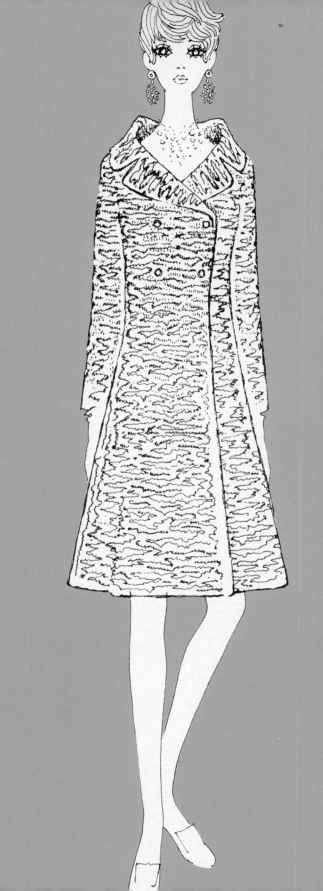

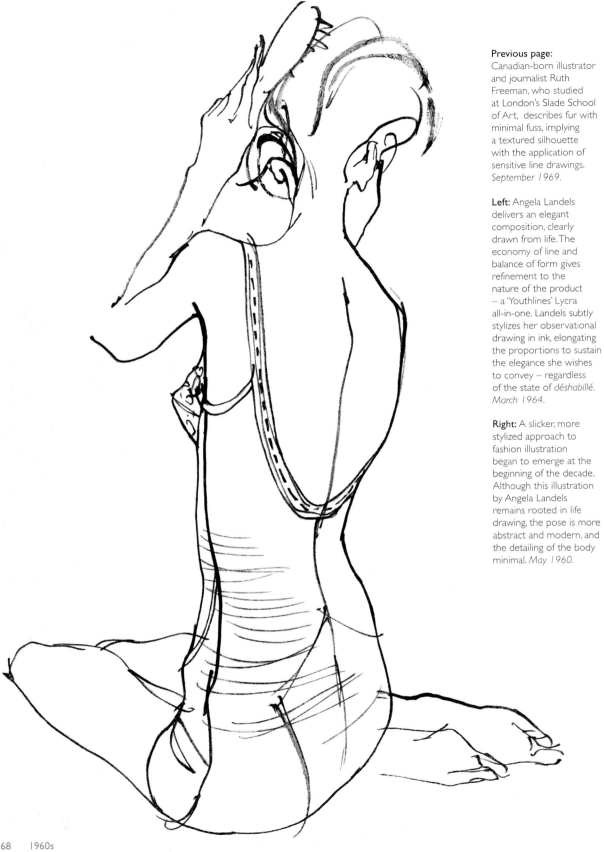

Previous page:
Canadian-born illustrator
and journalist Ruth
Freeman, who studied
at London's Slade School
of Art, describes fur with
minimal fuss, implying
a textured silhouette
with the application of
sensitive line drawings.
September 1969.

Left: Angela Landels
delivers an elegant
composition, clearly
drawn from life. The
economy of line and
balance of form gives
refinement to the
nature of the product
– a 'Youthlines' Lycra
all-in-one. Landels subtly
stylizes her observational
drawing in ink, elongating
the proportions to sustain
the elegance she wishes
to convey – regardless
of the state of *déshabillé*.
March 1964.

Right: A slicker, more
stylized approach to
fashion illustration
began to emerge at the
beginning of the decade.
Although this illustration
by Angela Landels
remains rooted in life
drawing, the pose is more
abstract and modern, and
the detailing of the body
minimal. *May 1960.*

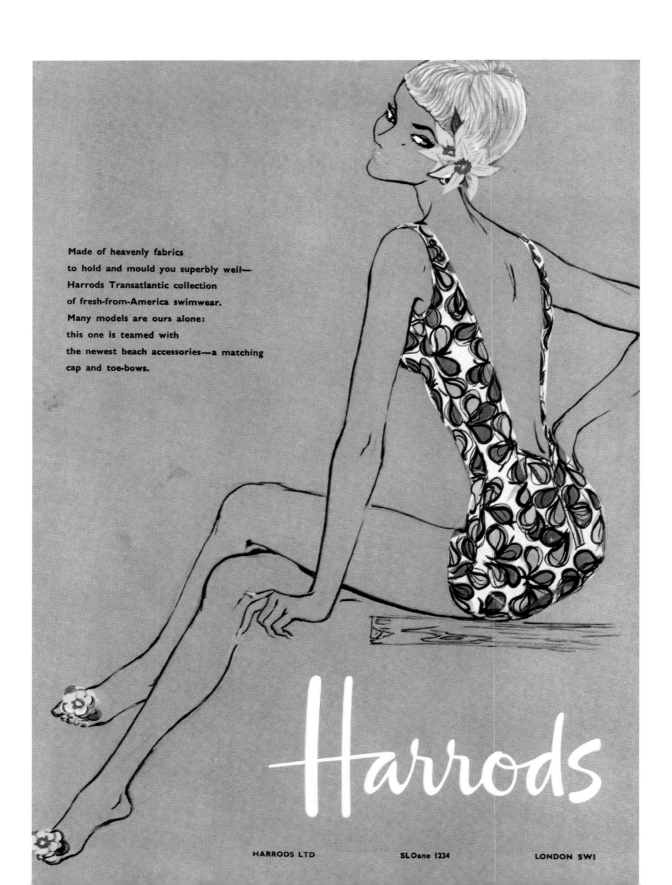

Made of heavenly fabrics
to hold and mould you superbly well—
Harrods Transatlantic collection
of fresh-from-America swimwear.
Many models are ours alone:
this one is teamed with
the newest beach accessories—a matching
cap and toe-bows.

Harrods

HARRODS LTD   SLOane 1234   LONDON SWI

Left: The illustrator has emphasized the salient points of the sales pitch – 'heavenly fabrics to hold and mould you' and 'matching cap and toe-bows' – by making efforts to define the items with greater graphic clarity. In this instance however, defects in the articulation of the figure drawing detract from the overall impact. *May 1960.*

Right: Women were relinquishing structured foundation garments in favour of more modern soft, unsupportive underwear. Illustrators such as Landels, therefore, attempted to imbue the product with a youthful, energetic glamour. *March 1964.*

Left: The garment is set against a tonal backdrop, while the tweed of the tailored suit is textured and flecked in black. The grown-up glamour of this carefully crafted suit is drawn with impeccable detailing. *October 1965*.

Right: Although the central figure illustrates a bra and pantie-girdle designed for Peter Pan by Oleg Cassini – Jacqueline Kennedy's favourite designer – the fashion currency is limited to the mature market. The style of all the illustrations is coherent with the garments depicted, having more in common with the late 1950s, rather than the incipient youth explosion of the 1960s. *March 1964*.

Far left, left and right: Drawn
and cut-out figures, which
have been produced with line
and wash. *October 1965.*

Left: In this illustration from 1964, Juliet Glynn-Smith pays little heed to anatomy but lavishes many pen and pencil strokes on suggesting the textiles. The shift dress on the right is clearly knitted and the pinafore dress on the left is probably woven hopsack linen. At the same time, the stylized floral design of the blouse has enough information to suggest that it references the Art Deco movement that underwent a surge in popularity during this period. *January 1964.*

brunetta

Above and left: Adopting a style of primitivism, Italian illustrator Brunetta chooses to define the forms of this eccentric array of garments by heavily documenting the patterning they contain, rather then outlining the specific contours of the figures. *June 1965.*

Left: In an attempt to make the accessory relevant in an era of youthful informality, the glove manufacturers Dents present a multi-coloured and patterned array of gloves in a lively and eye-catching manner. *December 1965.*

Right: The stark, poppy red silhouette of this illustration dramatizes a fairly generic knitted two-piece by Braemar. The head and hair are used as emblems of topical fashion – but old-school glamour rather than new-wave ingénue. *October 1965.*

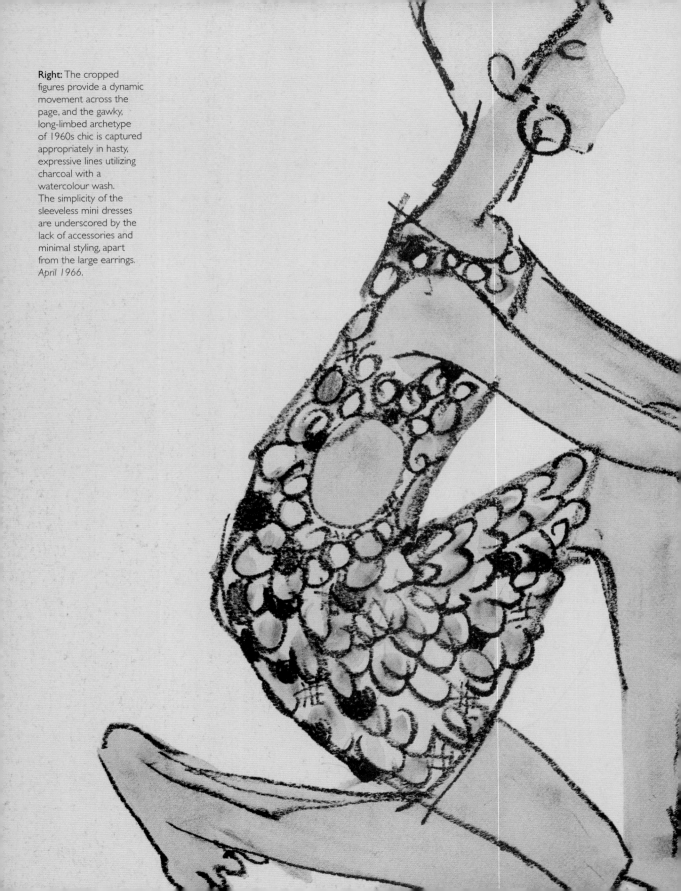

Right: The cropped figures provide a dynamic movement across the page, and the gawky, long-limbed archetype of 1960s chic is captured appropriately in hasty, expressive lines utilizing charcoal with a watercolour wash. The simplicity of the sleeveless mini dresses are underscored by the lack of accessories and minimal styling, apart from the large earrings. *April 1966.*

Right: Combining the optical effects of black and white with the revival of interest in Art Deco that occurred during this era, the models are portrayed with the small, neat head, the kohl-rimmed eyes and elongated body of the 1930s vamp. The differing textures of the garments are rendered as a flat pattern, rather than following the lines of the body. The scale of the hat veiling suggests that the drawing has been reduced from a larger size, a technique frequently deployed by illustrators to create a graphic edge to the image. *January 1966.*

Left: In an age of youthful revolution, the traditional values of fashion – longevity, classic design, and discreet good taste – are illustrated here with correspondingly traditional drawing skills, based on life drawing and executed in immaculate detail. The texture of the tweed suit is rendered by 'frottage', a technique invented by the Surrealist, Max Ernst, which involves taking rubbings from various uneven surfaces. *October 1967.*

Right: French style is implied in the title Gigi and in the evocation of the model's Bardo-esque updo hairstyle, in an attempt to render a thermal vest and knickers with an aura of glamour. *October 1966.*

Lux Lux
charms
your most
feminine
feelings

GIGI

BRI
NYLON
**STRETCH
LINGERIE**

Soft snug fashion underwear in six delightful colours. Illustrated, bra-style Vest and Pantaloon trimmed in frothy angel lace, selling at about 13/11 and 12/6. Match with Cosytop and Brief, about 10/6 each.

**LUX LUX LIMITED
GLOSSOP, DERBYSHIRE**
Telephone Glossop 2105
London Showroom: 45 Albermarle St.,
Telephone MAYfair 3663

THE SNOW SHOW

Left: skinny chevron-quilted beige nylon anorak clings snugly at hipline and wrists. Invisible zip. pockets in side seams. Michèle Rosier for V de V. at Aqua-Sprite, 5 Cale St. 21 gns. *Near right:* dead straight stretch gaberdine anorak with black knitted collar and cuffs. Bright yellow and six other colours. Bernard Altmann, 17½ gns. to order at Aqua-Sprite. Gaudy Clothes, Cheltenham. Black ski pants available, 12 gns. *Far right:* pop-printed featherweight wind jacket in black and white Rhovyl padded nylon lined in the same fabric. Louis Feraud at Henry Ours, for Gordon Lowe, 173/4 Sloane St. £30 9s. Henry Ours pants in Super Elastiss, 13 gns. also exclusively for Gordon Lowe.

Above: An ebullient semaphore, signalling frolicsome youth and reckless confidence, is created in this striking double-page spread of anoraks and ski pants. Even the text box is thrown akimbo to express juvenile *joie de vivre. November 1965.*

Above: The 1960s 'dolly bird' mediated through the 1930s vamp. The cigarette holder and cloche hat belong to the latter decade; the pose on the right is archetypal 1960s – the mini-skirt required an artless gamine, knee-together pose. *January 1966.*

Far left: Providing a guide to dress lengths, Ruth Freeman illustrates her own text with cleverly superimposed figures and textured tights. *May 1968.*

Left: Brunetta exploits the effect of monochrome textures, utilizing lines of various widths and density to convey texture and pattern in this series of whimsical drawings that combine a quirky combination of 'Op' and 'Pop' art influences. *February 1968.*

brunetta

This form-following underwear does so much for you,
it's a shame to waste such devastating appeal on your mirror.
But if you don't have a husband to tempt,
you can tantalise the males and still stay modest
by showing off the latest mini-pantaloons
under your mini-skirt!

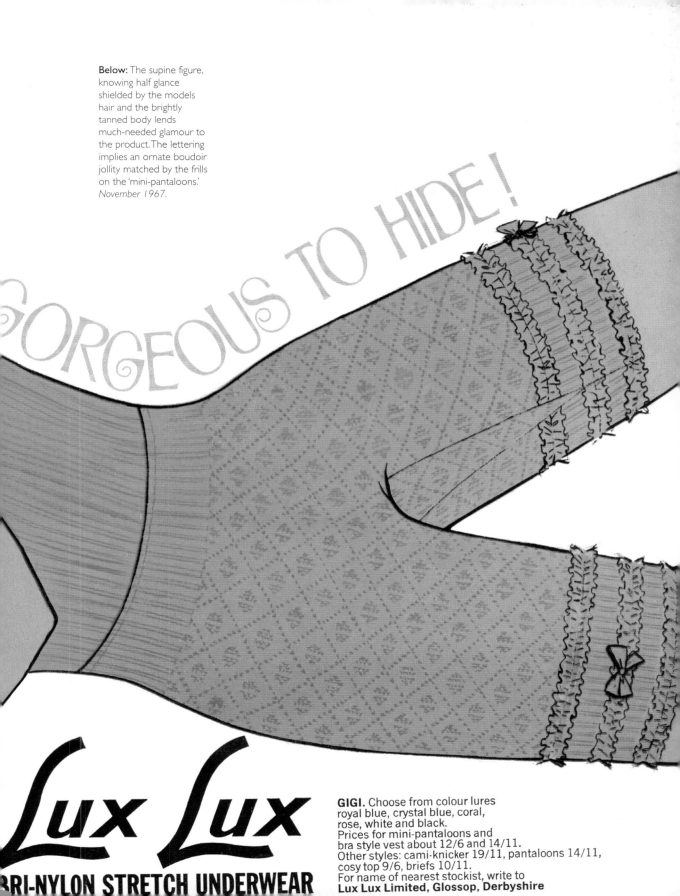

Below: The supine figure, knowing half glance shielded by the models hair and the brightly tanned body lends much-needed glamour to the product. The lettering implies an ornate boudoir jollity matched by the frills on the 'mini-pantaloons.' *November 1967.*

GORGEOUS TO HIDE!

Lux Lux
BRI-NYLON STRETCH UNDERWEAR

GIGI. Choose from colour lures royal blue, crystal blue, coral, rose, white and black.
Prices for mini-pantaloons and bra style vest about 12/6 and 14/11.
Other styles: cami-knicker 19/11, pantaloons 14/11, cosy top 9/6, briefs 10/11.
For name of nearest stockist, write to **Lux Lux Limited, Glossop, Derbyshire**

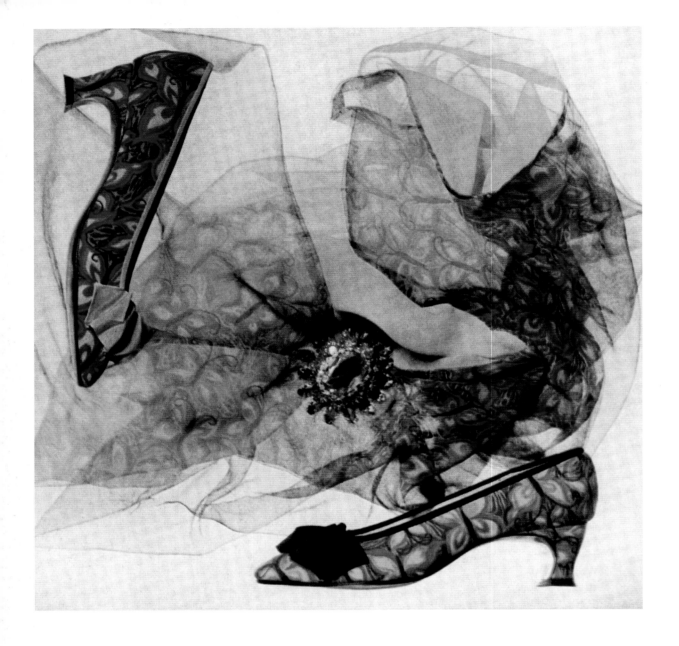

Above: In this painterly illustration, Peter Deal is strongly influenced by Leon Bakst's work for the Ballets Russe, such as the costumes for *Scheherazade*. Even the cast of colours would sit well with this vein of Orientalism. The careful rendering of transparency adds a sense of swirling motion to the composition of diaphanous printed scarf, opaque patterned pumps and the jewelled brooch with its the reflective qualities. *April 1965.*

Right: In 1966, London's Victoria and Albert Museum exhibited the work of Aubrey Beardsley and, together with Henri de Toulouse-Lautrec and Alphonse Mucha, was one of the three formative influences on the graphic design and poster art of the period. The animated figures on the dark background, the colour palette and the ornate lettering in this illustration are all in the style of Toulouse-Lautrec. *February 1968.*

The Honolulu Apron.

Palm Beach Lilly.

Galey&Lord

Design by Lilly of Palm Beach. Fabric by Galey & Lord. 1407 Broadway, N.Y., N.Y. 10018, a division of Burlington Industries

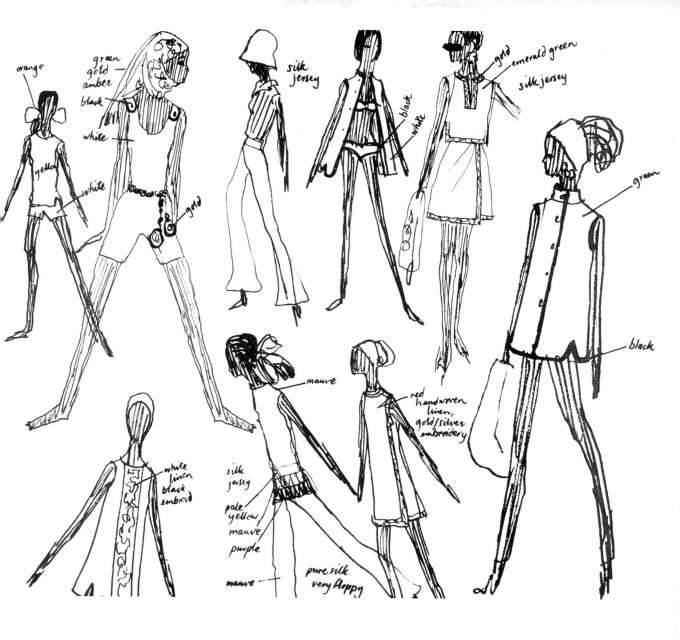

Labels on illustrations:

orange

green gold amber

black

white

white

gold

silk jersey

black white

gold emerald green silk jersey

green

black

white linen black embroid

mauve

silk jersey

pale yellow

mauve

purple

mauve

red handwoven linen, gold/silver embroidery

pure silk very floppy

Left: The influence of the poster art of Toulouse-Lautrec is unmistakable in this illustration for summer shifts. The tumbling auburn locks, striped mini dresses and the flirtatious wielding of the parasols by the energetic, dancing models are superimposed on a lime yellow background and framed by the ornate lettering. *March 1968.*

Above: In sharp contrast to the *croquis* of the previous decade (no live model has been used in these illustrations), these felt-tip rough sketches provide a shorthand interpretation of the body, the stylized forms providing just enough information on the minimalist garments. *February 1969.*

Following page: The youthfulness of the illustrated figures belies the nature of the heavily structured foundation garments worn during this period: in the 1960s girls wore little more than a pair of pants and an unstructured bra. The heavy line that delineates the body also outlines the garments; a finer line provides the garment details. *September 1966.*

Sun Set

Left hand page, left to right.
Towelling headband by Jer-Sea.
Daisy earrings, matching necklace
and bracelet by Corocraft.
Towelling wrapover dress by
Baltrik. Towelling shoulder bag
by Medusa. Sandals with daisy
by Elliott. Straw sombrero at
Mexicana. Turquoise silk scarf by
Richard Allan. Cotton top and
skirt edged in braid at Mexicana.
Silk scarf by Richard Allan.
Blue perspex sunglasses by Paul
Stephen. Bikini with perspex
straps by Emmanuell Khanh.
Plastic bangle by Plush Kicker.
Red and white platform shoes
by Ravel Studio. Right hand
page, left to right. Orange
towelling turban by Jer-Sea.
Black and striped knitted
wool bikini at Browns.
Bangle and ring by Plush
Kicker. Red leather, cork-
soled clogs by Elliott.
Towelling hat by
Bermona. Pink silk scarf
by Richard Allan.
Rose-tinted glasses by
Christian Dior.
Towelling top and
shorts by John Craig.
Pink Indian bangle
at Liberty's. Very
long two-tone
chiffon scarf by
Christian Dior.
Brown-framed
sunglasses
with ear
ornaments
by Adrien
Mann.
Towel-
ling
swim
suit by
Jer-Sea.
Silver
sandals by
Charles
Jourdan.
For stockists
and prices
see page 92

Previous page: Lush with air-brushed splendour, these figures denote a sybaritic, narcissistic attitude, whether looking straight out of the page or averting their gaze. The almost photographic quality of the drawing is offset by some clumsy areas – the figure on the right is out of proportion, while the figure to her left appears to float above the ground. *March 1969.*

Left: Master of all he surveys, the figure in this illustration concedes an element of dandyism so prevalent of the era in the nipped-in waist of the single-breasted jacket. The image pastiches the pose and style of a Victorian engraving in the heavy lines and liberal use of cross-hatching; a technique by which the artist constructs areas of shadow by crossing lines at various angles. *September 1969.*

Fortnum
&Mason

Fortnum
&Mason

perfection: Ungaro Parellèle collection   exclusively at Fortnum & Mason, Pic

Jean Muir thinks   then designs   and creates a fashion role of pure allure.
Enter the Intellectual Seductress. Panther-like grace in a long, lean look.
Colours sombre, yet potent, slithered closely over the body.
Eve, circa 1970, wittily playing serpentine print against the real thing.
Print blouse £30. 10. 0., scarf £8. 10. 0., black trousers £22. 0. 0.
Black python waistcoat, £45. 0. 0. Entire put-on exclusively at Fortnum & Mason
Jean Muir at Fortnum & Mason, Piccadilly, London W.1.

Above left: Prevailing attitudes prohibited women
from wearing trousers in most restaurants and hotels,
but they became an increasingly acceptable item for
daywear. The elongation of this figure is emphasized
by the perspective of the long, low shadow, the dense
blackness of which is in marked contrast to the sensitive
pencil line that describes the model's trouser suit.
September 1969.

Above right: The trailing multi-patterned head scarves
and snakeskin-printed waistcoat subvert the tailored
trousers and crisp blouse into faux hippie mode in this
illustration for British designer Jean Muir. The frottage
technique has been used to provide the checked
texture of the trousers. *October 1969.*

Right: Cartoon-like androgynous figures inspired by the graphic style of the day are superimposed on Pop-art motifs such as stars, stripes and explosions of bright primary colours. The double-seaming described on the garments supports the architectonic fashion silhouette prevalent during the era. *October 1967.*

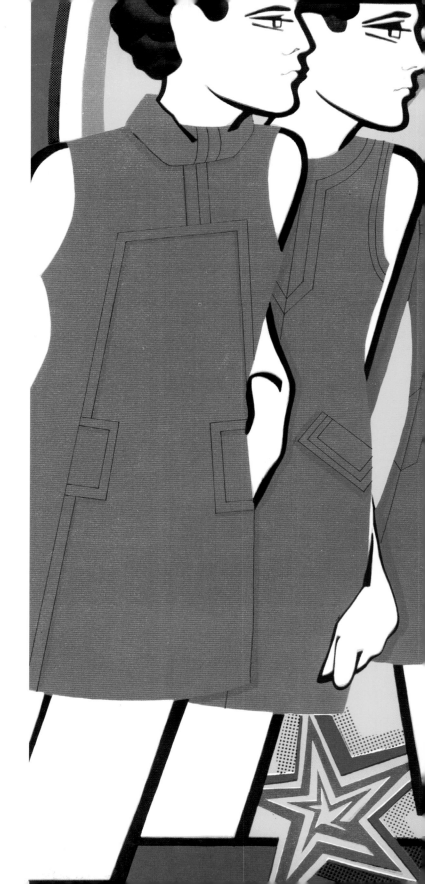

Left and right: The simple architectural line of the clothes corresponds to the pared-down directness of these line drawings in wash and felt-tipped pen, in which the illustrator concentrates on the carefully described hairstyles rather than on the functional details of the clothes such as side seams, bust darts and openings. The adjustment to the arm of the figure on the left is an example of 'pentimento', a correction made by the artist during the early stages of the work. *April 1967.*

Below: The psychedelic garb of velvet trousers and mirrored kaftans worn by the 1960s hippie is only hinted at in this illustration of men's knitwear by the inclusion of the patterned neckerchiefs and low-slung belts. Rendered in felt-tip pen and flat wash, the rugged texture of knitted garments is described in pencil. *November 1969.*

Right: The invention of the modern felt-tip pen by Yukio Horie of the Tokyo Stationery Company, Japan, in 1962, provided another tool for the illustrator. A smooth adherence to the surface of the paper, easy to manipulate and with instant impact, it has subsequently remained the medium of choice for the drawing of *croquis*, including these by fashion journalist Philippa Chelsea. *September 1967.*

Index